Diving For Hidden Treasures

GW00777497

Uncovering the Cost of Delay in Your
Project Portfolio

Johanna Rothman and Jutta
Eckstein

Diving For Hidden Treasures

Uncovering the Cost of Delay in Your Project Portfolio

Johanna Rothman and Jutta Eckstein

ISBN 978-1-943487-08-0

Practical **ink**

Contents

CONTENTS

Acknowledgments

We thank Stefan Krahe for his photography as our cover art. Thank you, Robert Woods for suggesting such a great title for our work.

Why do we care about the value of the project portfolio?

We play organizational games with estimates, budgets and goals. And, we use them to make serious decisions in organizations. Value is how we reconcile these problems. If we make decisions by value, we change how we rank the backlog for the iteration, we change how we organize the project portfolio, and we change how we fund the projects for the organization.

How do we find the value? What feeds into the value? Cost of delay is part of it. Creation of market share is part of it. Waste is part of it. Investment is part of it. You will need to determine value for your organization by looking at all of these things and discussing them.

However, if we try to create a goal with an estimate, either the goal is wrong or the estimate is wrong. People estimate so they know it will fit into the iterations, instead of looking at what they need or they estimate a project so it fits the overall portfolio. People are forced to estimate to fit the date. We see this at the iteration, project, and project portfolio levels.

How do we value different projects and programs in the project portfolio? One common way is to use estimation. Especially for large programs, estimation is costly and wrong. The estimate becomes the target, the plan. The estimate is a trap for the eventual project or program. The estimate prevents feedback or continuous learning. The complexity of today's projects and project portfolios puts an extra burden on decision making.

Estimation is insufficient for evaluating the project portfolio. We need to use value. Value is more difficult, and adheres to the agile

1

principles. Learn how to evaluate the project portfolio by adhering to the core agile values.

Planning and Controlling Complex Projects

Jutta Eckstein

I have been working on large and complex agile projects for more than 20 years. Typically planning and budgeting are based on trying to predict how development will turn out. Very often the stories are estimated by the development team, but the budget for the whole project is independent from those estimates. Especially for complex projects this leads most often to (unwanted) surprises. However, learning about Daniel Kahneman's and the Beyond Budgeting folks' work helped me a great deal in better understanding how planning, estimating and budgeting relate and why the traditional approaches don't work. Of course, we all know how this works in the small, how to plan and steer a project by iterations. Yet, how will you decide in favor or against a project, how do you define the budget for starting a large project, and how do you know how your tiny iterations (across many feature teams) fit into the long-term project goal? Please note, I'm not talking about small or regular projects, I'm talking about projects with 50-300 developers, taking for example 3-5 years to finish or comparable large product (line) development.

Prediction is not possible

Daniel Kahneman, winner of the nobel prize in economics although he is a psychologist, came to the conclusion that most of the things that are happening, are based on coincidence: One of the examples he gives refers to the past history — chances stood 50:50 that the embryo who became Adolf Hitler would have been female. Who knows how this would have changed the past hundred years in the world? This means predicting complex events is not possible.

However, Kahneman collected as well work from colleagues who researched in the same field in order to verify his point. For example Philip Tetlock, also a psychologist from the University of Pennsylvania collected more than 80.000 political and economic predictions. Note that the people who came up with those predictions actually make a living from predicting the future, so we are talking about real experts! Problem was that those predictions were worse than applying just the normal curve of distribution to the prediction. Yet, when proved wrong, hardly anyone acknowledged that his predictions were wrong, almost all of the experts came up with excuses or reasons why they believe they were actually right yet the timing was wrong without providing any reasoning for what kind of timing would have been right.

In another study, Terry Odeon, a finance professor at the University of Berkeley analyzed approximately 10.000 broker results consisting of 163.000 trades. The interesting aspect with brokerage is that for every trade there must be someone who believes that it will be better to sell e.g. the stock and someone else believes buying it would be better. Yet, both traders are typically regarded as experts in the field. In this analysis Odeon found that on average the stocks sold performed 3.2% better than the ones bought.

The last example, I want to mention is one based on Kahneman's own experience. He used to work for the Israel army. There he created a test which he used with his group to evaluate candidates for the officer career. You can imagine probably very well that kind of test - next to interviews, people had to solve some tough problems where they had to build something, get over another thing and this way it became apparent who is taking the lead, who is opposing, who is a good team player and so on. Based on observing the applicants during this test, Kahneman and his team developed always a high confidence for the further qualification of the people.

However, the feedback they received from the commander every few months was that their evaluation was only a tiny bit better than blind guess. Interesting fact is, that neither Kahneman nor his colleagues changed their approach or rather the conclusions from their observations based on this feedback. When seeing an applicant taking the lead it was still obvious to them that this will be the perfect candidate for the officer career. They were just too convinced about their impression that changing the conclusions seem to be impossible for them.

So what can we learn from those studies? There are two really important lessons to be learned:

- First, predictions will always be error-prone, just because the world "or rather any complex event" is not predictable.
- Second, high subjective confidence (as experts often show no matter if their confidence refers to recommending soldiers for an officer career or to estimating a project) is no sign of accuracy, it is only a sign that the expert has a coherent story. High confidence (sometimes as well called intuition) can only be trusted if you are acting in a stable environment.
- And there is actually a third lesson in Kahneman's research I didn't bother verifying this with a study because this is the foundation for iterative development: In contradiction to long-term trends, short-term ones can be predicted with fair accuracy as long as they are based on previous behaviors, patterns and achievements.

Beyond Budgeting to the Rescue

Beyond Budgeting (see http://bbrt.org[1] and http://www.bbtn.org/[2]) is a development driven by CFOs from different companies. They

---

[1] http://bbrt.org
[2] http://www.bbtn.org/

were unhappy with the effect budgeting had on the success of the respective company. The typical experiences and you might be able to relate to those are two-fold:

- Imagine somebody is asking for a specific budget for e.g. a project and then the project turns out to be cheaper. Being afraid that next time when asking for money only getting half of it, the remaining money will be spend anyway (although not for the original purpose). Thus, this isn't really contributing to the company's success.

And now imagine that someone asks for a specific budget, but then the market changes, which might mean he would need twice the budget. Well, he didn't ask for it ahead of time and therefore it's not possible to act according to the market needs. And again, the company's success suffers from the original budgeting.

Based on these experiences, the Beyond Budgeting people developed different kinds of principles and recommendations. Neither of those necessarily mean to get rid of budgets but to use them more flexible. For example, negotiating annually on the budget is regarded as inflexible. Therefore, the recommendation is to use for example a rolling budget, which means to verify every month where the money is spent best. An alternative to the rolling budget is the event-based budgeting, thus whenever some changes are happening, the budget will be reconsidered.

One of the most important insights of beyond budgeting is in my opinion to differentiate between target and forecast. The rationale is that every goal should be ambitious whereas the forecast (or estimation) is a way to close the gap to the goal. Now if both -target and forecast- are forced into one number the result is that either the target isn't ambitious anymore or the estimation is a deception.

Applying Beyond Budgeting

In order to decide in favor or against a project or product, somebody has an idea and then asks maybe a senior developer or even a team for a number in terms of effort and therefore cost. The problem is that at this point in time not much is known about the project and therefore the estimations are not really solid. Sometimes it's sales who comes up with an estimation without consulting development and then the decision is made. (And of course no matter who comes up with this first estimation it's always assured toward development that this number will not be taken serious and it will be adjusted once we know more!)

Given the findings of both Kahneman and Beyond Budgeting this approach isn't helpful. First of all it ignores Beyond Budgeting's differentiation between target and forecast. Second, in contrary to Kahneman's insights the approach assumes that complex projects can be predicted and third, it suggests against Beyond Budgeting's advice to approve the budget upfront.

What we need instead is first to clarify the overall goal. In order to not rely just on one group of experts (remember Kahneman's findings), I recommend performing this clarification in a diverse group. Depending on the project this group should be assembled by e.g. the customer, marketing, sales, product management, and at best supported with scientific methods in order to find out the real needs of the market as Lean Startup suggests. The outcome of this clarification is not an estimation but the definition of the business value that the company (or the customer) imagines to achieve with the project. Looking at the business value shifts the mindset from what it will cost to what we will gain. The business value can be defined by discussing it, using a Delphi session or as I have done in the past as well by using a variation of planning poker. For the latter instead of using estimation numbers for driving the discussion, the group members use numbers referring to the business value.

Then instead of asking how long it will take, the same diverse group has to find out how much they are willing to spend (based on the business value they previously came up with). Naturally this group will struggle (at first) in a similar way coming up with a number for the investment as the developers do when coming up with an estimation. Yet, the business has to decide where it wants to spend the money. From the development point of view, everything can be made in a really high-sophisticated and expensive way (which typically is very much in line with the working ethics, speaking e.g. of clean code) but at the same time things can be implemented at low cost (which could lead to unmaintainable code). Yet, the business has to decide how much the business value is worth (which can result in asking for a cheap solution). This does not mean that there is no responsibility left for the developers in terms of planning - their task is to ensure business understands what impact a cheap (or expensive) solution might have. Consequently, estimation is not in the focus at that point. It is the decision on the business value and the investment the company wants to make that has to drive the development. Again, these drivers are created by the business and not by the development. Some teams just do the opposite, by asking development to not estimate on the story level only, but as well on the epic level (by estimating e.g. in T-Shirt sizes) or on the project level. Yet, trying to answer how much the project, epic, or story costs (or how long it takes) focuses on the wrong question. Again: the appropriate question to ask is how much is this worth and how much are we willing to invest in it.

This way, both the business value and the investment define a framework for steering the development. At best, both should be broken down to the story level yet at least to the epic level. For large projects, we have made good experiences planning on at least three levels. The highest level is the overall project plan (often called roadmap). The next level is the release plan, with a release enduring three months at maximum. Thus, before starting a release, the epics for this release will be defined in terms of business value and investment. At the level of the iterations (the lowest level), the business value and investment for the stories is defined before the classic iteration planning happens (i.e. sprint planning one and two). Depending on the lengths of the release (and as well on the complexity of the project), we sometimes have the need for what Mike Cohn once called a "rolling lookahead plan." Thus, we look into the business value and investment of the stories not only for the upcoming iteration but as well for the next two or even three iterations. Planning on these different levels provides the possibility for the business to define the business value and investment first at a coarse grained level and then iteratively making it more fine-grained. Defining it on a fine-grained level right away is on the one hand for large projects impossible and one the other hand not useful because it is very likely that the business value (and the reasons for the investment) will change over time.

Applying this approach at the different levels ensures that development is always driven by business value and investment and not by estimation. I still recommend to conducting a planning poker session for estimating the stories as a development team. Yet, this is done for creating the knowledge about the stories within the team, but not for driving development. Thus, the resulting estimation numbers are only important for driving the conversation, especially when team members at first disagree on the estimation numbers the discussion on their different assumptions will create a shared understanding of the story. This way, the estimation is still helpful for the team but it will not drive the planning. The prioritization and the definition what is in and what is out of scope of development is based on what the story is worth in terms of business value and investment (and not in terms of how long it will take or of how much story points it costs). Thus, business value together with investment provides a guideline for the prioritization and for the development. For example, if a specific story has assigned a low investment and doesn't provide a high business value the priority of the story has to be questioned (independent of the story points estimated for it). Furthermore, it should be obvious that for such a story the development team should look for the cheapest solution and if there is none then the story has to be exchanged for one that provides a higher business value (and / or the company decides to make a higher investment).

As well the business value and the investment have to be verified regularly, similarly to the rolling or event-based budget. For example, at least after every other iteration look at what has been learned from the stakeholders (e.g. what kind of changes will provide a competitive advantage), from the market (e.g. where do we need to invest in order to create a higher business value) and as well from development (e.g. what advantage does a specific technology provide). Then analyze how this influences the business value and / or the investment on the different levels. It is helpful to first take a look at what this means for the release plan - often it affects only this level, so there is no need for taking it to the overall project level. Yet, at some times it has such an impact that as well the roadmap will be influenced by the changes. Certainly when defining the business value and investment for the upcoming iteration (and if applicable for the rolling lookahead plan, i.e. for the next two or three iterations) the new lessons learned should be taken into account.

In general, if the customer's competitive advantage is really our focal point then the business has to be driven by the business value. Thus far in agile development we have been talking about the business value but we just considered the priorities (often additionally under consideration of the estimates). Yet only the combination with the investment ensures that we always maximize the value in the customer's interest.

Conclusion

Recent findings in research together with the insights from Beyond Budgeting prove what many of us have experienced: Accurate forecasts aren't possible because the world is not predictable (especially not nowadays). Getting a prediction from an expert with high confidence just means that the expert has a coherent story and not that the accuracy of the prediction is high therefore instead of asking an expert, ask a diverse group of people.

For not falling into the trap of mixing estimation and planning, define a business value and come up with an investment you are willing to put into this undertaking and use these values for planning. These values help you to decide on the decision for or against starting a project and help you to come up with a roadmap for the project (or product) and a release plan. So especially on the project and on the epic level the business value and the defined investment will drive development.

Short-term predictions are possible, therefore measure the velocity and take this into account when planning the next iteration. The feedback of the iteration and of the stakeholders helps to improve the handling of both, the business value and the investment. So on the one hand the business value and investment steer the iteration and on the other hand the feedback of the iteration helps improve the business value and the investment. Or in other words: the roadmap influences the release plan which influences the iteration and vice versa - the result of the iteration feeds back into the release plan and this in turn into the roadmap. Therefore, the business value and the investment are treated as a rolling budget that is revisited regularly so all lessons learned will be considered.

References

Daniel Kahneman, *Thinking Fast and Slow*, Penguin Books, 2011

Bjarte Bogsnes, *Implementing Beyond Budgeting*, John Wiley & Sons, Hoboken, NJ. 2009

Beyond Budgeting Roundtable (Homepage of Beyond Budgeting): http://bbrt.org[3]

Mike Cohn, *Agile Estimating and Planning*, Prentice Hall, Upper Saddle River, NJ. 2006

---

[3]http://bbrt.org

Why Cost is the Wrong Question for Evaluating Projects

Johanna Rothman

I read Sayonara Sony: How Industrial, MBA-Style Leadership Killed a Once Great Company[4], and was struck by how the company appeared to make decisions—what will make us the most money now?

If you make your project portfolio decisions based on money, estimated cost, you too will have Sony's problems. This is why cost is the wrong question to ask. You want to ask the value question, "How much value will this project provide?"

This is not a return on investment question. That's a prediction question. You can't answer that question either.

When you use cost as the "which project should we fund?" you can guess right. But you guess based on what you think the market will buy, not what you decide is the right strategy for your company. Big difference.

This is why you want a mix of projects in your project portfolio: Projects that keep the lights on; projects that keep cash coming in; and projects that are innovative, that have the power to transform your organization. And the problem is this: in software, you often can't tell which one is which. This is why agile or lean is so wonderful. You don't have to be able to tell.

---

[4]http://www.forbes.com/sites/adamhartung/2012/04/20/sayonara-sony-how-industrial-mba-style-leadership-killed-once-great-company/

If you use incremental budgeting and an agile approach to your project portfolio, and an agile/lean approach to your projects, you can pivot when you need to.

Now, you might need to do a quick SWAG (Scientific Wild Tush Guess) for an order of magnitude estimate for your project. Is this project bigger than a breadbox? Is it smaller than a space station? That's not a *project* estimate. That's a SWAG, an order of magnitude estimate. You do a SWAG with a few people in under an hour. Two hours max.

For the project portfolio, you make the evaluation decision based on your best guess of the project's comparative value to the organization. This is why it's so helpful to be able to deliver something in a short period of time, such as 2-6 weeks, when the project portfolio people will want to reevaluate the portfolio again.

Oh, and those Sony engineers? The ones who were laid off when Sony couldn't keep their commitment to lifetime employment? Some of them went to LG[5]. You know, the company that you probably bought your flat screen TV from? All I know, is that every hotel I stay in has an LG TV. In our house, we have (smaller) LG TVs.

When you use value to make project portfolio decisions, you decide on the most valuable project. If you change your mind, you don't change the people. You change what the people do—you flow work through the team. Is this more difficult with hardware? Of course. Is it impossible? No.

People want autonomy, mastery, purpose. (Yes, this is from Dan Pink.) Give it to them. Tell them what is the number one project. The number two project, etc. Tell them what is not funded, and why. They will work for you, to make it happen.

---

[5]http://www.bloomberg.com/news/2013-09-26/sony-s-lost-generation-risks-push-to-restore-walkman-mojo-tech.html

Estimation is Insufficient as a Basis for the Project Portfolio Evaluation

Johanna Rothman

Many management teams want an estimate for projects and programs in order to evaluate the project portfolio.

If you fall for estimation as your way of valuing projects in the portfolio, you are doomed to fail. Why? Because you are trying to predict the cost or the date when you know the least about the project. I guarantee you do not have a full backlog. I guarantee you do not know everything about the product. I bet you don't have everyone on the program. You could spend umpty-ump Iteration Zeros and not get to an accurate estimate. It doesn't matter.

You have to use value as the basis for ranking the projects in the project portfolio.

You don't have to go into the project portfolio ranking blind, especially if you use agile approaches. You can say, "Do an iteration (or two or three) and create a walking skeleton. What does that tell us?"

This works if your iterations are short, as in one or two weeks. If your iterations are longer than two weeks, this doesn't work. Sorry, you are now in contract negotiation.

Now, based on the teams knowledge (or some small number of the teams knowledge), do a SWAG estimate of how big this program is. I timebox this step. "Is this program worth doing?" is a valid question. This is different than an ROI (return on investment) analysis. This is asking, "If we spend time on this program, will we get something valuable that is releaseable to customers before we've spent all our money?"

The "is this program worth doing" is a different question than either "can we release every iteration" or "what is the ROI for this program". The "worth doing" question is a question of magnitude. The "can we release every iteration" is a question in the small. The ROI question attempts to estimate every item in the backlog, the backlog that in my experience is bound to change, which makes estimation moot. (I have seen teams waste team-years in estimation. Yes, I have.)

If you use estimation as the basis for evaluating projects in your portfolio, you will miss potentially transforming projects. You will miss the projects/programs that have the capacity to push you light-years ahead of your competition. Why? Because you can't estimate them. Why? Because you haven't done them before! You have no freaking clue how long they take. You can lie and SWAG them. Or, you can provide a walking skeleton and keep re-estimating them.

Or, you can do what we've done since time immemorial: provide interim deliverables at frequent milestones and show your progress. Agile allows us to do this very well. So does staged delivery, because it's an incremental (not iterative) lifecycle, which is why I like it. You build the product and show your progress. If you are from the Engineering side of the house, this is concurrent engineering.

When you do show progress, you build trust. You can collaborate.

A Focus on Continuous Value

Jutta Eckstein

Focusing continuously on the business value isn't possible!?

How can you maximize the business value in an agile project if you have to consider as well non-technical requirements. The focus of an agile approach is to maximize the business value constantly. Yet, how this can be done leads often to misunderstandings. Frequently people are asking how the following can possibly contribute to the business value:

- Fixing bugs?
- Refactoring?
- Non-functional requirements in general?

Those questions are motivated by some key misunderstandings: Namely that most people think solely about the end user if they think about business value. This way they ignore that next to the end user there are other kind of groups that have an interest in the system and for whom the business value has to be maximized as well.

Therefore, you have to clarify at first who are the stakeholders for the system. All these diverse groups (among them for example operations, maintenance, or other developers who are building on your system) have to be considered. You can do so by collecting as well their user stories and by asking them for feedback regularly. The key is to prioritize the different stories of the diverse stakeholders - this is the reason why the task of the product owner is extremely challenging (and why it is almost impossible to find somebody who can take that role amongst your customers). This means the product owner has to weigh the demands of the diverse stakeholders and to come up with the right balance through prioritization.

The foundation for the weighting lies in clarifying the following:

- For whom does a particular story provide a business value (or rather: who is the stakeholder for a specific story)?
- How can you measure that business value?

The measurability is typically defined in terms of acceptance criteria and ideally implemented as acceptance tests. If the stakeholder and / or the acceptance criteria of a story are unclear no matter if this is a new story, a bug, or a refactoring an agile team can hardly maximize the business value. Or in other words: only the definition of the stakeholder and the acceptance criteria allow a team to keep the focus of an agile approach, which is maximizing the business value continuously.

Cost of Delay Due to Not Shipping on Time

Johanna Rothman

Do you know about the Cost of Delay? It's the way to think about the revenue you can lose plus the cost of continued development.

One of my managers many years ago had a back of the napkin approach to cost of delay.

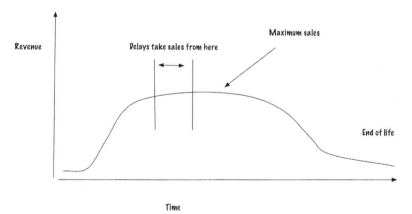

Cost of Delay, Back of the Napkin

"Johanna, we want to ship this product in the second quarter this year. We estimate it will take us a quarter to ramp up sales. We think there is a lifetime sales of about five years for this product. Any delays in our shipment will not push our sales figures to the right. They will remove our max sales from the middle. Got it? We have to make our ship date."

I got it.

There weren't too many of us developers in that organization. We all knew what our job was: to release on time, and make sure the product was usable. The product didn't have to be perfect. The product had to be usable, because we could release fixes *if we needed to*, but we had to climb that sales ramp to get to that max sales point.

We worked on one project at at a time, until it was done. Then we went to the next project. We worked on that project. None of our projects was very long. Why? Because we needed to realize revenue. You can't realize revenue with a product-in-a-box if you don't ship it.

We didn't ship too many fixes. Oh, not because we were perfect the first time. We asked each other for review, and we found problems, so we fixed them inside the building. Before we shipped. Because the cost of not shipping on time was too great.

When you delay your release and don't ship on time, you miss the revenue from the *maximum* sales times. Take your delay in weeks, and remove the revenue weeks. That's your cost of delay, back of the napkin approach.

You can go through more serious calculations. Troy Magennis of Focused Objective[6] talks about a "compounding impact" on other projects. I am sure he's correct.

But even if you said, "Every week we slip, we lose at least a week of revenue from our *maximum* sales week of revenue," do you think people would notice?

How do you release on time? You fix scope (ha!). You have release criteria[7]. You have shorter projects,[8] because they are easier to estimate and deliver. You use an incremental or an agile lifecycle[9],

---

[6]http://focusedobjective.com/cost-of-delay/

[7]http://www.jrothman.com/blog/mpd/2004/03/release-criteria-define-what-done-means.html

[8]http://www.jrothman.com/blog/mpd/2011/11/estimating-the-unknown-dates-or-budgets-part-4.html

[9]http://www.jrothman.com/2008/01/what-lifecycle-selecting-the-right-model-for-your-project/

so you have more predictability about your release.

This post is the simple idea of not shipping on time. But what about when you have competing projects and not enough people? Look for the Cost of Delay Due to Multitasking, next.

P.S. After I wrote this post, I realized I was not living this post. (Why do you think I write? It's not just for you. It's for me too.) I published the incomplete Predicting the Unpredictable[10]. I have another essay or two to release. But if I don't release it, you can't read it and get any value from it, can you? The point: if you don't release your products, your customers can't get any value. Hat Tip to @jlottsen who said in a tweet, "you have to release it, or no one can use it, and you can't realize any revenue at all". Very true.

---

[10]http://www.jrothman.com/books/predicting-the-unpredictable-pragmatic-approaches-to-estimating-cost-or-schedule/

Cost of Delay Due to Multitasking

Johanna Rothman

In Cost of Delay: Not Shipping on Time, I introduced you to the notion of cost of delay. I said you could reduce the cost of delay by managing your projects: have shorter projects, using release criteria, or selecting a lifecycle that manages the risk.

Sometimes, you don't have short projects, so projects get backed up, and your managers ask you to work on several things at once. Or, the managers can't decide which project is #1. Somehow, you end up doing several things "at once." This is the multitasking problem, and this is the cost of delay in this part.

You know me, I hate multitasking[11]. The costs[12] are significant. But those are just the costs of multitasking on the work you are doing now. That has nothing to do with the cost of delay to your *projects*.

In Manage It!,[13] I have this nice picture of what happens when you try to multitask between two projects.

---

[11]http://www.jrothman.com/blog/mpd/2013/07/mutlitasking-think-again.html

[12]http://www.jrothman.com/blog/mpd/2006/11/costs-of-multitasking.html

[13]http://www.jrothman.com/books/manage-it-your-guide-to-modern-pragmatic-project-management/

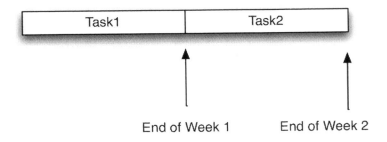

End of Week 1   End of Week 2

Two Tasks or Projects

Imagine you have two projects. Each of them should take a week. Hey, they're short projects. I'm trying to illustrate a point.

You can deliver one of them at the end of the first week. You can deliver the second one at the end of the second week.

But, imagine you have to multitask between them. Instead of being able to deliver anything at the end of the first week, you can't deliver anything at all until the second week. And, depending on how much context switching you do, you might not be able to deliver anything until sometime during the third week. The blue boxes show the time lost due to context switching.

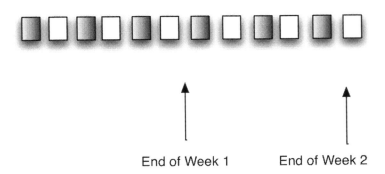

End of Week 1   End of Week 2

Effect of Multitasking Delay to Delivery

This is a huge cost of delay due to multitasking.

How do you calculate this?

"Big" is not quantitative enough for some people. This is where using some of the tools from the people who do this for a living might be good.

I've always drawn a picture like this and explained, "I don't know how to estimate the time in the blue boxes. The blue boxes are the delay times. I can't estimate them, because everyone else is delayed by multitasking on their projects, too. Sometimes, it takes me an entire day to get an answer to a question that should only take me an hour to get an answer. All I know is that "ideal" time is irrelevant to actual time. And even calculating using relative estimation is hopeless. That's because we are multitasking. All of our estimations are out the window because we are multitasking.

"The amount of time we spend working on a project might be accurate. It's the wait time that's killing us. I don't know how to estimate that."

What I've done before is take a two- or four-week window, and ask people to write down their *predictions* of what they thought some task would take. Then, I ask them to write down, as they spend their time on each task, how much time they actually spend on each task. Now you can compare the prediction to reality.

Remember that all of the context switching and wait time is the time you need to remove from the maximum sales revenue, had you released the product.

This is very difficult to do. It saps the morale of the people doing the work. They quickly realize how often they go back to the same thing, over and over and over again, making zero progress, trying to realize where they are. Do not do this for more than a four-week window. If you must do this, label this an experiment to obtain data. Explain you are trying to obtain actual work time, context switching time, and wait time. Let people label the time as they will.

The managers will be astonished by how little time the technical staff spend on real work. They will be amazed by how much time the technical staff spend on context switching and wait time. This is why managers think technical staff are bad at estimation. Who can be good at estimation when they are multitasking?

The problem is this: the cost of delay due to multitasking is real. It's invisible to most people, especially management. It's not just the cost of the blue boxes in the picture above. It's the fact that nothing gets out of your organization until the end of Week 2 or later. Remember the back of the napkin in Cost of Delay: Not Shipping on Time? Even if you use that calculation, you can see you are losing revenue left and right due to multitasking.

Remind the managers: Remember that all of the context switching and wait time is the time you need to remove from the maximum sales revenue, had you released *any* of the products.

Can you use this as an argument for your managers to end the multitasking and manage the project portfolio[14]?

Cost of delay due to multitasking is real. What would you need to know to calculate it in your organization?

---

[14]http://www.jrothman.com/books/manage-your-project-portfolio-increase-your-capacity-and-finish-more-projects/

Cost of Delay Due to Experts

Jutta Eckstein

Often companies rely on experts, because they will solve the problems quicker than generalists. However, it is often overlooked that relying on experts has a tremendous cost of delay. In order to make this transparent, imagine you are a problem and want to get solved (I know this sounds weird, but stay with me for the moment). Typically you have to line up in a problem queue of a dedicated expert who can solve those kinds of problems. Because there is not only one problem and not only one kind of expert, there are now different problem queues for different experts.

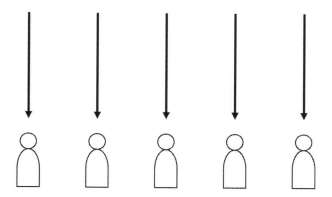

Different Problem Queues for Different Experts

Now, if one of the experts struggles, his queue will get longer and longer:

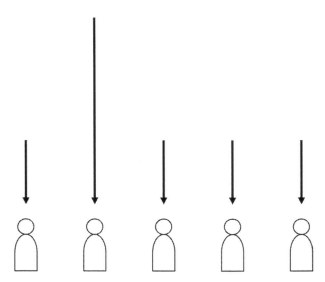

One Expert Struggling

This means, it could happen that some problems are solved quickly - because these problems were lucky ending up by the "right" expert or rather in a queue where the problems are currently easy. And some problems are hardly ever solved, just because one problem created a bottleneck or rather a blockage in one of the queues. Please note, that none of the problems will be solved depending on urgency, business value or any other kind of priority. They will all just be solved in the order by accidentally ending up in a specific queue. If you instead of relying on sole experts establish cross-functional teams who can help each other and solve problems jointly, you can reduce this cost of delay significantly. You will end up having only one problem queue with a steady flow rate.

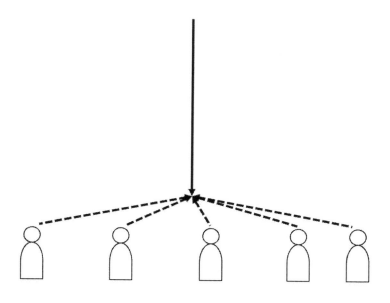

Steady Flow Rate

The flow rate will be steady because every member of the team just pulls the next problem that waits in the queue. So only now you can prioritize the queue with the effect that the problems will as well be solved in priority order.

Please note I am well aware that there are a lot of circumstances where it will be hard if not impossible to have generalists only. The circumstances very often are that the required expert knowledge differentiates so much that a single person can't master it all. However, this does not have to lead as it is often does to educating people so they are mastering one expertise only. Because the more specialized the individuals are, the higher your cost of delay will be. Instead your goal should always be that as many people as possible will master as many different knowledge areas as possible. A good rule of thumb is that in a team every individual should master about three different knowledge areas and every knowledge area should be mastered by about three team members.

Cost of Delay Due to Making Things Right

Jutta Eckstein

Most developers I know are proud of their work. They want to build up a reputation individually, as a team, as a company, as a profession. So whatever they work on they want to make things right. There are many ways of doing things right:

- Ensuring there is no technical debts
- Adhering to clean code
- Implementing the story so it is absolutely fault-tolerant
- Dealing with all eventualities of the business the functionality is addressing

This is all really good and as well important. However, it is not always required. It might not be required, because the client does not need to have a 100%-fault-tolerant system or because the budget for the system does not allow investing in clean code (now). Maybe it is important to ship the functionality, so that the client can use it right away and everything else is of secondary importance. Maybe the business strategy is to sell functionality first and quality later. Oh, I'm not saying that this is my preferred strategy, but some companies rely on exactly this strategy by selling cheap functionality first which implies a limited budget (this is how they win the bid) and then they sell expensive maintenance later. If this is not obvious to the developers they might not only delay shipping the functionality because the implementation is not good enough according to their standard. But moreover, their behavior might as well ensure that the company runs out of business. Because the company can't survive on the low bid for shipping the features, if nobody will buy the expensive maintenance later. You think this scenario is made up? Actually I know more than one company which ran out of business because their developers shipped products that were better than the business strategy implied.

If you are in a market that is highly innovative, you have a similar problem. In such a market you have to provide the features quickly in order to stay at the top of innovation. You can later invest in improving the quality. But at first, it is important to ship the features so your clients can see and experience where you are heading. I have seen as well companies running out of business because the development department refrained from shipping because the product was not good enough. The competitor's product was quality-wise much worse, but they shipped. So they stayed in the market.

So cost of delay due to making things right or gold-framing the features can kill not only the product but the whole company. Therefore, the maximum investment (based on the return on investment) for providing the requested functionality has to be clear for development. Only then can the implementation take the investment into account. Yes, sometimes this means to ship functionalities although you would still like to improve them - yet if you keep improving the functionalities you might never be able to ship them.

Therefore, sometimes it might be less important to ask the developers for an estimate of how complex the functionality is (or how long it will take to build it), but more important to ask the business side how much they are willing to invest in it. Otherwise shipping the product might be unnecessarily delayed.

Cost of Delay Due to Technical Debt

Johanna Rothman

One of the big problems in backlog management is ranking technical debt stories. It's even more of a problem when it's time to rank technical debt projects. You think product owners have feature-itis[15] problems? Try having them rank technical debt projects. Almost impossible.

But if you really want the value from your project portfolio, you will look at your impediments. And, if you are like many of my clients, you have technical debt: a build system that isn't sufficiently automated, insufficient automated system tests, too many system-level defects, who knows what else.

If you addressed the build system, and maybe some of the system tests, if you created a timeboxed technical debt project, you could save time on all of the other projects in this code base. All of them.

Imagine this scenario: you have a 2000-person Engineering organization. It takes you 3 *weeks* (yes, 21 calendar days) to create a real build that you know works. You currently can release every 12-18 months. You want to release every 3-6 months, because you have to respond to market competitors. In order to do that, you have to fix the build system. But you have a list of possible features, an arm and a leg long. What do you do?

This client first tried to do more features. They tried to do features in iterations. Oh, they tried.

By the time they called me, they were desperate. I did an assessment. I asked them if they knew how much the build system cost them.

---

[15]http://www.jrothman.com/blog/mpd/2011/06/do-you-have-feature-itis.html

They had a group of a 12 people who "supported" the build system. It took at least 10 days, but closer and closer to 20-25 days to get a working build. They tried to estimate the cost of the build in just this group of people: 12 people time 21 days. They did not account for the cost of delay in their projects.

I showed them the back of the napkin calculation in Cost of Delay: Not Shipping on Time, and asked, "How many releases have you postponed for at least a month, due to the build system?" They had an answer, which was in the double digits. They had sales in the millions for the maximum revenue. But they still had a sticking point.

If they funded this project, they would have no builds for four weeks. None. Nada. Zilch. And, their *best* people (whatever that means) would be on the build project for four weeks.

So, no architecture development, no design, no working on anything by the best people on anything other than the build system. This company was convinced that stopping Engineering for a month was a radical step.

Does it matter how long your iterations are, if you can't build during the iterations and get feedback?

They finally did fund this project, after about six months of hobbling along.

After four weeks of intense work by 16 of their smartest people, they had an automated build system that anyone in Engineering could use. It still took 2 days to build. But that was heaven for everyone. They continued the build system work for another month, in parallel with regular Engineering work to reduce build system time.

After all the build system work, Engineering was able to change. They were able to transition to agile. Now, Engineering could make progress on their feature list, and release when it made sense for their business.

What was the payback for the build system work? Almost im-
mediate, Engineering staff said. When I asked one of the VPs, he
estimated, off the record, that they had lost more than the "millions"
of dollars of revenue because they did not have the features needed
at the time the market demanded. All because of the build system.

People didn't plan for things to get this way. They got that way a
little at a time, and because no one wanted to fund work on the
build system.

This is a dramatic story due to technical debt. I bet you have a story
just like this one.

The cost of delay due to technical debt is real. If you never look
at your technical debt and see where it impedes you, you are not
looking at the value of your entire project portfolio.

If you eliminated a technical debt impediment, would that change
one of your costs of delay?

Cost of Delay Due to Doing the Wrong Things

Jutta Eckstein

Often teams are so busy implementing the requested functionality, so they have hardly time to stop, think, and reflect about what they do and how they do stuff. I have often heard after a completed (or stopped) project the insight (accompanied with a deep sigh) that if we would have only talked about this and that earlier or if we only would have made this minor change in time then our life would have been so much easier.

Yet, while working on the project on the one hand it often does not occur to the involved persons to also consider alternatives and discuss those. And on the other hand, even if this does occur to them then very often the response is but we don't have the time to concern ourselves with these things. In German there is a saying that supports this attitude: We don't have time to sharpen the saw, we have to saw. In Texas this is expressed similarly: We can't build a fence, we have to chase the cattle.

Thus, especially under pressure we keep doing stuff, but we hardly ever stop and think of better ways of doing this stuff. And we hardly ever stop and take time for improving the situation before we go back to work. Often this leads to Cost of Delay Due to Technical Debt). Very often the technical debts have the same source - that is we keep working on the features (because this is what needs to get shipped and what the customers are pushing for) although the technical debt is the reason why we can (hardly) really ship the features.

Therefore, in order to not delaying your project you need to stop from time to time and concentrate on what needs to be improved (or fixed) in your environment or in your way of working. Then take again time to really improve and fix these things. As a result you can benefit from faster delivery.

This is the purpose of (regular) retrospectives in agile development. Too often I have seen people skipping them under project pressure, because they don't have time for stuff like that yet exactly if you don't have time, you need to do things like this (maybe for figuring out why you don't have time). So sometimes this means, you have to go slower in order to become faster.

Cost of Delay Due to Indecision

Johanna Rothman

Here's a problem I encounter often. A middle manager calls me, and asks for an estimation workshop. I ask about the environment. The manager tells me these things:

- The developers meet their dates and the testers never do (this is not an estimation problem)
- The project starts on time, and the project staff comes in close, but not quite on time (this might be an estimation problem)
- The project starts off late (this is not an estimation problem)

When the developers meet their dates but the testers never do, it's almost always a couple of things: Schedule Chicken[16], or technical debt masquerading as done in a waterfall project.

If the project starts on time and it's close, it might be an estimation problem, assuming no one is multitasking.

But if the project starts late, this is not an estimation problem. This is a cost of delay due to management indecision.

Wouldn't it be nice if you could say,

> *A lack of planning on your part does not constitute an emergency on my part*

---

[16]http://www.jrothman.com/2005/01/dont-play-schedule-chicken/

to your managers? Well, just call me the Queen of the Career Limiting Conversation. This is why managers are supposed to manage the project portfolio[17].

When I hear the plea for the estimation workshop, it's for these reasons:

- The managers have received estimations for the work, and they don't like the estimates they have received.
- Someone other than the project team did the estimation two years ago. They know the estimate is out of date, and they need a new estimate.
- The managers still can't make a decision, because they are trying to decide based on ROI, date, or cost or some sort of hard to predict quantitative measure, rather than on value[18].

The managers are, ahem, all tied up in their shorts. They can't decide, which is a decision. They don't fund the potentially transformative projects or programs. They go with the safe bets. They do the same projects over and over again.

If they get lucky, they choose a project which is small and has a chance of success.

How do you discuss this cost of delay? You ask this question:

- *When did you first start discussing this project as a potential project?* or
- *When did this project first go on our backlog?*

That provides you the first date you need. This is your next question:

---

[17]http://www.jrothman.com/books/manage-your-project-portfolio-increase-your-capacity-and-finish-more-projects/

[18]http://www.jrothman.com/blog/mpd/2013/10/why-cost-is-the-wrong-question-for-evaluating-projects-in-your-project-portfolio.html

- *When did we actually start working on this project?*

You want to see how long it takes you to consider projects. It's okay to consider some projects for a while. The difference between the time you first start discussing a project and the time you start working on it is your *management cost of delay.* I just made that up. I bet there's a real name for it.

- *What is the difference in those two dates?*

Project lead time is the time you started discussing a potential project and the time you *finished* it. Project cycle time is the time you started a project and the time you finished it. Yes, we normally discuss lead time and cycle time for features. But sometimes, it makes sense for projects, too.

If you release projects, not features, and you have managers who have decision problems, they need to know about this cost of delay. Because the project lead time will take time out of your maximum revenue. The longer that lead time is, the more it will take.

The worst part is this: how much value does the project have, if the project lead time is "too long?"

What can you do?

1. Track your project lead times. Decide how much time a project can spend on the backlog in the project portfolio before you decide to transform or kill it. Yes, I am serious.
2. Shorten all your projects, so you release something at least every six months, or more often. That provides you more capability in assessing your project portfolio and frees teams for more work.
3. Move to an incremental lifecycle or an agile approach.

I didn't say it was easy. It's healthier for your organization.

Who do you think can measure this cost of delay in your organization? What do you think might have to change to make this cost of delay visible?

Cost of Delay Due to Not Starting

Jutta Eckstein

As Fred Brooks once so wisely stated: How does a project get to be a year late? One day at a time. Sometimes a project is not started eternally Due to Indecision. And sometimes the decision is made early to start the project but the team is hesitant to really get started.

There are few common smells pointing to delaying the start:

- Sprint Zero: The Sprint Zero is scheduled before all regular sprints as a means for preparing whatever needs to be prepared (e.g. the product backlog, the infrastructure, etc.). Therefore, teams are asking for a Sprint Zero because they (think they) have to prepare this and that before they can actually start. Moreover, the Sprint Zero is often prolonged - so sometimes this Sprint is actually longer than all subsequent Sprints. Instead of prolonging the Sprint Zero occasionally there are many Sprint Zeros. The concept of Sprint Zero most often is an excuse for not having to start and deliver right away. Certainly there are cases where you need to set up stuff. Yet, what prevents you from considering the preparation work as a delivery? And moreover what is the reason for not proving that the preparation and set-up is actually useful and working by delivering as well a (very) small functionality?
- Definition of Ready: The Definition of Ready is an agreement on the upfront definition or description of a story (this is also true for regular requirements), so the developers know enough for implementing that functionality. The request for

43

the Definition of Ready undermines the original idea of agile development that stories are a promise to talk. To talk about the functionality once it will be addressed. Thus, originally a story was meant as a token that helps business people and developers to talk about the required functionality. In contrast, the Definition of Ready is typically used by the developers to refuse to working on a story, because the story hasn't been described in an acceptable way. Thus, instead of discussing the functionality together and implementing it, stories are now thrown over the wall between business and development a couple of times. Obviously this leads to delaying the delivery of that functionality.

Both principles - Sprint Zero and Definition of Ready are actually delaying tactics and create as such cost of delay. Therefore, before requesting next time a Sprint Zero, think about if you really need it. And if you do, come up with a goal and acceptance criteria for that sprint as you do with any other sprint. Maybe it will help you already to not call it Sprint Zero but instead your first sprint. This way it will be easier to ensure that you will deliver your sprint goal.

In case your team asks for a Definition of Ready, in the team discuss what kind of problem you want to solve with this definition. And moreover, ask yourself why business and development can't work on the stories jointly.

Taking both to heart ensures to refrain from delaying the start the start of the project and of the implementation of the stories.

References

Fred Brooks. *The Mythical Man-Month.* Addison-Wesley, Reading, Mass. 1995

Cost of Delay Due to Features in Progress

Jutta Eckstein

If you take the idea of shipping early and often seriously, you want to work on one feature after the other and ship the features as soon as they are done. In agile development this approach is typically managed by making the status of the features (or stories) visible on a board. The status of a feature can be one of the following:

- To do (or: planned)
- In progress
- To be verified (or: to be reviewed or something like that, which is actually a sub-status of in progress)
- Done (or: shippable maybe even: shipped)

I have seen many cases, where the features are in progress, but they hardly move forward from there. One team was honest enough to introduce for such circumstances another status called "on hold". It should be obvious, that everything that is not progressing ensures the cost of delay to increase. If you are in the situation where features are started but not finished, the first you should do is visualizing this fact. This can be done with the introduction of that "on hold"-status as the other team did, or by providing an overview of the status of all features with a cumulative flow diagram. The larger the stack for the features in progress is, the higher your cost of delay is:

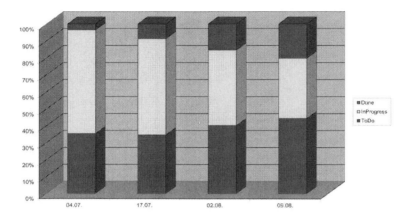

Cumulative flow diagram shows features in To do (red); In progress (yellow); Done (green)

Next you should look for the reason for that state. Conducting a retrospective on that topic might help you to both understanding the reason for the situation and creating actions for improving it.

The reason I see the most often is that features are cut in a way, so they can hardly be finished. If you collaborate with other teams, it could mean that you have the Cost of Delay Due to Other Team's Delay. If only one team is involved, it could mean that for accomplishing the feature a decision is required. The decision might have to be made within the team, e.g. do we want to implement this feature using framework X or Y; or external to the team, e.g. is there a budget to buy framework X? Or it could mean that there is a bit missing, e.g. we want to use framework X for the implementation of the feature, but the supplier needs to fix something beforehand; or we need to adjust the database (or the data) in order to complete the feature.

In all of those cases, it seems the feature is not cut right. Features should always be cut in a way so they can be completed without any dependencies. The stuff a feature is (with the wrong cut) dependent on, should be defined in a separate feature and then every feature can be completed independently. Thus the clue is to resolve dependencies already when slicing features - otherwise you create costs of delay.

Cost of Delay Due to Releasing Later

Jutta Eckstein

Your team might be ready to ship early and often, but your company's release strategy might prevent the system to enter the market. Some companies have release strategies that allow to ship systems only once per year.

Of course the cost of delay is obvious: the system sits there, ready yet nobody is buying and using it. Thus the system doesn't provide any return on investment, because of the release strategy.

Yet even worse there is another cost of delay added, which is the later a team receives the feedback from the market (changes, enhancements, bug fixes) the longer it will take the team to incorporate this feedback. This is plainly due to the fact that the fresher your memory is regarding the system the easier it will be to change it. The more time has passed since you built the system, the more time it will take you to get into your original thinking again. Thus, you can look at this cost of delay as well as a specific variation of Cost of Delay Due to Multitasking.

Of course documentation and tests help—yet nothing helps better than releasing and getting feedback timely.

Cost of Delay due to Unsupportive Infrastructure

Jutta Eckstein

Often teams deliver frequently, yet the system can't be shipped or does not provide the required quality, because the infrastructure does not support frequent delivery. We have seen different variations of this problem:

- You are working in an environment that requires an expensive test infrastructure. Because of the high expense, the environment is not easily accessible. You will only get specific slots during the year for testing your system. This is closely related to Cost of Delay Due to Releasing Later. The question remains if the company saves more money by not providing sufficient support or by releasing earlier and making money from the newly developed product.
- You have great developers on your team, but hardly any testers. Thus your team is creating great features and the developers try to test them as good as possible yet the knowledge about i.e. exploratory testing and the like are missing. Therefore, ever so often your customers detect quality problems in the field. This leads to unsatisfied customers and this leads sometimes in turn to fewer customers for your next releases. So in this example, the unsupportive infrastructure is created by the team that is not really cross-functional. It is very likely that it is cross-functional in terms of business and technology, yet not in terms of activities that are required in order to get features really done.

51

- You have a great team for building a system, but using the enterprise-wide tools (e.g. development tool), frameworks (e.g. for creating the UI part of your system), or architecture slow(s) you down. Some companies have this policy that all projects should use the same tools, frameworks, or underlying architecture. In one of projects I know of, the teams were required to use a development tool which was specialized for creating systems with a focus on highly-sophisticated user interfaces. Yet, the system this team was building did hardly have a user interface. So the development tool was on the one hand not of much help and on the other hand the team needed features of the development tool which did not exist. In a different company, all projects were required to build their product by using a particular framework. This framework was created for rich client technology. Yet this project created a system based on thin clients. Thus, for almost every feature the enterprise-wide framework was in the team's way. From the company's point of view this makes perfect sense, mainly because maintenance will get so much easier and as well moving people from one project to another does not create a high cost. However, the price for using enterprise-wide tools and technologies that are not serving the purpose of your system often put a much higher price tag to the product. Not only because it slows development down, yet also because it is frustrating for the team.

For avoiding this kind of cost of delay, you have to pay continuous attention to the infrastructure – both in terms of the people working on the system as well as on the environment that allows you to develop and deliver.

References

More on delays by enterprise-wide tools and technologies in:

Jutta Eckstein, *Agile Software Development in the Large: Diving into the Deep.* Dorset House, NY. 2004.

Cost of Delay Due to Other Teams' Delay

Johanna Rothman

Imagine you have a large program, where you have several teams contributing to the success of one business deliverable. You are all trying to achieve a specific date for release.

One team is having trouble. Maybe this is their first missed deliverable. Maybe it's their second. Maybe they have had trouble meeting their deliverables all along—they have "delivered," but the deliverables don't work.

Now, say you're halfway through the desired program time. You, as a program manager, can see that this program is in trouble. That one team is not going to make it. What do you do?

This is where you start talking to people and understanding what the *value* of everything is.

1. Does the program need everything on that team's backlog?
2. Does the program need everything on that other team's backlogs?
3. Does the program product owner understand the cost of delay?
4. How about the sponsors for the program? Do they know what's going on?

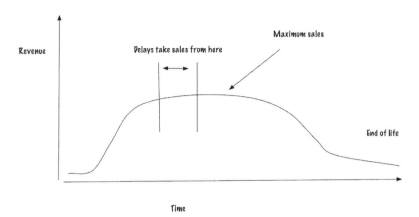

Cost of Delay, Back of the Napkin

Take out your back of the napkin calculation and show it to anyone who will listen.

Does the team understand the problem of lateness, as we discussed in Cost of Delay: Not Shipping on Time? They might. They might be overwhelmed by the technical difficulty of what they are doing. Maybe their stories are huge. Maybe they aren't so hot at agile. Maybe they aren't working in an agile way. There are 1001 reasons for this problem. If you are a manager of any stripe, program manager, development manager, whatever, you are responsible for understanding first, not yelling. (I often see senior development managers, VP Engineering encountering this, not realizing that they are the program managers in this situation.)

Does the program product owner really need everything in their backlog? It's time to consider how little can that team do,[19] and still deliver something of value. Or, it's time to consider how little other teams do and still deliver something of value. Or, it's time to rejigger who is doing what. Otherwise, you are going to lose the money in the middle of the revenue stream.

Are the teams working by layer, front end, middleware, back end,

---

[19]http://www.jrothman.com/blog/mpd/2003/05/how-little-can-you-do.html

instead of through the architecture?

Something has to change in this program. You are not going to make the desired date. This problem is a larger case of the not shipping on time problem, but it's not just one team. It involves more teams. And, with a program, it involves more money. It's almost always a bigger stake.

This is when you want to start considering cost of delay for features. Yes, not just for releases, but for features.

Each feature has value when you deliver it at a certain time. Before a certain time, it might have more or less value. After a certain time, it has less value.

Who knows when that time is? Who can make these decisions in your organization. Sometimes that person is called a product owner, a product manager, or, gasp, a customer. Sometimes, that person is called a Marketing Manager or Director, or even a CEO. Rarely is that person called a developer or tester, or even a development manager or test manager or an Engineering manager or CIO or VP of Engineering. Sometimes the product development side knows. Almost never does the product development team know by themselves.

If you make decisions as a cross-functional team, product development and marketing, you can get the best of both worlds. You can learn about the technical risks—especially good if the team is having technical problems. You can learn about the cost of delay risks—especially good from the customer perspective. Now, you can make a decision about what to do for the good of the program.

You have to optimize for the program's throughput, not any one team's throughput.

In my world, you work with the team: do they want to stay together? Are they working well together, and having a tough time technically? If so, the team has many options:

- The team can ask for technical help from another team (get an architect/designer to work *with* the team)
- The team can split their backlog among several other teams, to give them a fighting chance.
- If the team is not working well together (and they will tell you if they are still storming), offer them a chance to split.
- Or, you can facilitate a better working relationship so they can work well together.

If you don't ask the team, you don't know what's wrong.

The problem with this cost of delay is that it's tricky to discuss, it's tricky to estimate, and it's tricky to fix. It's real. I bet you've seen it.

I would take out the napkin and remind the team that their delay costs the entire program. I want to help them remove that delay.

If you are using a waterfall approach to your programs, this cost of delay is invisible until the end of the program, when testing occurs. Why? Because that's when you start to see features emerge.

If you are using an agile approach or at least an incremental lifecycle, you will start to see this much sooner, and you can do something about it.

Cost of Delay: Why You Should Care

Johanna Rothman

The real problem is this: Why should you care? Maybe you have a "sweet spot" in the way you start your projects or release them. "It just takes that long here." (That's the sign of a system impediment.)

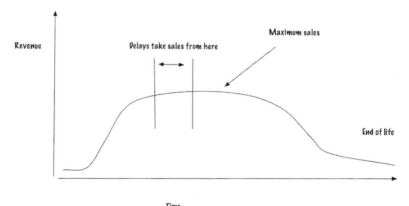

Cost of Delay, Back of the Napkin

Let me show you two pictures. The first you've already seen, the back of the napkin, where you see the effect on your potential maximum revenue.

Now, let's try to calculate that cost of delay.

The longer your delay, the more your cost of delay moves your curve to the right. The more sales you lose out of the *Maximum* potential sales.

The longer it takes for you to release, the more sales you lose from the maximum potential sales. You wait a month to release? You lose a month of max sales. You wait a year to release? You lose a year of max sales.

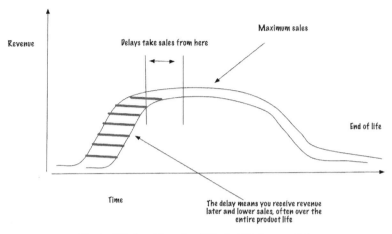

Cost of Delay, Showing Effect of Delay on Sales

That's right. Do those numbers start to look big and scary now?

You not only have aggravation and impediments in your current project from the delays from multitasking, technical debt, indecision, slowdowns from other teams, you lose the potential revenue from maximum potential sales, every week you don't release.

Now, I am not saying you should release horrible product. Goodness knows, we have enough of horrible product that barely works or doesn't work at all out in the field. I want to see great products! The idea behind this picture is so people understand that it is worth their while to consider change.

You can change to shorter projects and release something useful faster. (See Manage It! Your Guide to Modern, Pragmatic Project Management[20])

You can change to agile or incremental lifecycles so they can see

---

[20]http://www.jrothman.com/books/manage-it-your-guide-to-modern-pragmatic-project-management/

progress and release something useful faster. (See What Lifecycle? Selecting the Right Model for Your Project[21] and Manage It! Your Guide to Modern, Pragmatic Project Management[22] for an in-depth discussion of lifecycles. You have more options than just waterfall and agile.)

You can adopt a more reasonable approach to the project portfolio, and make decisions more frequently. (Does anyone really think project portfolio decisions last a year? Come on.) (See Manage Your Project Portfolio: Increase Your Capacity and Finish More Projects[23])

You can consider paying off some technical debt. I used the build system in my example. I could have used automated tests or the thousands of defects some of you have in your defect tracking systems. It's whatever prevents you from knowing you could release on a "moment's" notice. I would like that moment to be under an hour. I bet for many of you, less than a day would be a huge improvement.

You can optimize for the entire project or program, not their feature or team. Too often, I hear, "My part is done." That does not matter. It matters what the entire team, project, or program finishes.

In my talks about project portfolio management, I am fond of saying, "It doesn't matter how many projects you start, it matters how many you finish."

With cost of delay, it matters *when* you finish them. Because until you finish them, no one pays you.

I have taken a high level approach to cost of delay in these posts. I wanted to simplify it so you and I could understand it, a zeroth approach, if you will. If you want more information, start here:

[21]http://www.jrothman.com/2008/01/what-lifecycle-selecting-the-right-model-for-your-project/

[22]http://www.jrothman.com/books/manage-it-your-guide-to-modern-pragmatic-project-management/

[23]http://www.jrothman.com/books/manage-your-project-portfolio-increase-your-capacity-and-finish-more-projects/

- Blackwanfarming.com[24]
- Focused Objectives[25]

Cost of delay is why you cannot take an ROI or use date or budget estimates to manage the project portfolio. This is why you must use value[26].

---

[24]http://blackswanfarming.com/

[25]http://focusedobjective.com/cost-of-delay/

[26]http://www.jrothman.com/blog/mpd/2013/10/why-cost-is-the-wrong-question-for-evaluating-projects-in-your-project-portfolio.html

Selecting a Ranking Method for Your Project Portfolio

Johanna Rothman

One of the most difficult parts of project portfolio management is deciding how to rank the projects—that is, determining which projects should be done now, later, and, most importantly, never. There are several ways to rank a project portfolio. Each is useful in specific situations and not so useful in others. But all share the same goal; namely, arriving at a single ranked list of projects.

> Dave, a CIO, gathered his directors together. "OK, everyone, listen up. We have too much to do. Everyone's multitasking, which means we're not getting anything done. Our projects are still late. We need to decide what projects we're going to do first, second, and third, and then stick with that, at least for a while." His directors looked at him as if he had three heads.

> "I'm serious. We'll rank our projects and see which ones are most valuable, do those, finish them, and then go on to the next project."

> "How do you propose we do that?" asked Tanya, a director. "We don't know what's most important to you or to the rest of the senior management team. In fact, we keep getting different messages. First, my calendar integration project is first, then it's the data integration project. Once last week, it was the performance project — but only for a day. I'm quite happy to rank the

projects, but how long do we think that ranking will last, and how can we do it?"

Dave frowned. "Well, we've got a chance to make some decisions, show how we made them, and make them stick just for a few weeks. That will give us a chance to finish some work and rerank, if we have to."

You probably share Dave's problem. You have too many projects to do at the same time, not enough people, and not enough projects finishing. If that's the case, it's time to consider ranking the projects your organization has. In this chapter, we will explore a number of approaches to ranking projects:

- Assigning projects a point value
- Assessing the risk of a project
- Reviewing the project context
- Using double or single elimination
- Ranking a project according to your organization's mission and values

So let's get started. First, list all your active projects—that's your project backlog. Now it's time to start asking the difficult questions.

Ask This Question First

Once you start ranking the projects, make sure you ask this question first:

Should this project be done at all?[1]

If there's no sponsor, no customer, and especially no identifiable value for the project, stop it.

Don't be afraid to not do projects at all, and especially *for now*. Project portfolio management is about making choices that guide the technical staff to finishing work on just the most important projects in the organization. If you can't make a compelling argument for finishing this project, put the project back on the project backlog for now. Or, add it to a parking lot [1], where you list the projects not under active consideration, but you don't want to forget about.

But more likely, the answer to *'should we do this project'* question is yes, and you need to proceed to ranking the projects. Ranking requires discussion among the sponsor, the customer or customer surrogate, and some description of project value.

Rank with points

Project value is the value of the project to the organization. If you could rank the projects with an ordinal ranking — as in, 1, 2, 3, and so on — your work would be done. But you often need more conversation than mere ordinal ranking affords. Points help you articulate the business value and provide a visible means of showing the relative business value of each project.

When you rank with points, you assign a number of points to a project, allocating more points to more valuable projects. Points represent business value. If you wanted, you could use dollars (or euros, or whatever you have), as in "How many dollars do we want to invest in this project?" Sometimes, that's difficult to do if you aren't sure how long the project will take or don't know enough about the features. When you're evaluating the portfolio, you may not have thought through all those issues yet. Using points as a way to rank projects separates the project funding question from the business value decision.

Separating project sizing from duration helps project team members make better estimates. In the same way, separating business value from funding allows managers to see what output they desire from the organization. If all the projects have a small number of points relative to each other, then no one cares much about the set of projects.

When you rank with points, you take a large number of points, much larger than the total number of projects. For example, if you have eight projects, take 10,000 points to start. Now assign a unique number of points to each project. If you have two very important projects, you cannot assign each of them 5,000 points. You can assign 5,001 points to one project, and 4,999 points to the other project. Yes, both projects are very important, more important than anything else you have in your portfolio. However, allotting 5,001 points to the first project says, "This project is the most important one." The 4,999-point project is next in line.

By assigning a unique number to each project, you show the organization which project is most important for now. If you allocate the same number of points to more than one project, the technical staff doesn't know which project is most important, and you don't have a project ranking. It's too easy for each person to make his or her own decision, which might be different from yours.

Table 1: A Ranked Listing of a Small Number of Projects

Project	Points
Project 1	3000
Project 2	2500
Project 3	1250
Project 4	750
Total Points	**7500**

You might not use all your points. For example, in Table 1, one organization with four projects only used 7,500 of their possible

10,000 points. If you don't use all your points, you may need to reconsider the projects you're trying to rank. If you don't have several projects that provide substantial business value, you may not be considering enough or the right kinds of projects.

As you proceed through the project ranking, you might realize that you want a larger point spread to show the rest of the organization how the projects rank against each other. In that case, you may need more points to clarify the ranking. See Table 2 for an example of a team that started with 10,000 points and wanted to show the rest of the organization how important Projects 1, 2, 3, and 4 were. Projects 5 and 6 are much less important.

Table 2: Ranked Listing of Projects where the decision-makers changed the number of points used to rank

Project	Original Points out of 10,000	Updated Points out of 20,000
Project 1	2000	5000
Project 2	1900	4000
Project 3	1800	3500
Project 4	1700	3400
Project 5	1600	1000
Project 6	1000	500
Total points	10,000	17,400

Points help you describe the relative importance of each project. If you need more points to describe the relative importance, use them. When you use more points, and have a larger difference between the most important and least important projects, project staff understand when to stay with one project.

When I introduce this approach to management teams, they ask, "What do the points mean?" I've had good results saying, "You have $10,000 to assign to these projects. How do you want to assign the money?" There are times, though, when linking project value with dollars isn't sufficient. In such cases, the managers will try to assess the risk of not doing the project and assign this risk a dollar value. One way or another, you need to link points to project value.

Table 3: Dave's Ranked Listing of Projects

Calendar integration	5000 points
Data integration	4000 points
Performance project	1000 points

Dave worked with his directors to use points to rank their projects. Their initial decision about their projects is shown in Table 3. But when Dave brought the ranking to his senior management team, they were concerned—wasn't the calendar project too risky to keep as the top priority? Senior management was concerned that if the entire IT group was stuck on the calendar project, nothing would get done. Dave and his team needed to address risk.

Rank with Risk

I bet you've heard things like "Don't do the risky projects—do the sure things." Well, that's great, but how do you know what a sure thing is? How can you tell what the return on a project will be?

You can't tell for sure, but you can learn a little about the risk and value of a given project, assuming you do just one iteration's worth of work on it. When you work on projects, feature-by-feature, inside a timebox, finishing features and showing demos as you proceed, you can learn more about the risk and the potential return. Once you've completed one iteration's worth of work and received feedback on the demo from a customer or customer-surrogate, you might have enough information to evaluate the project's risk. Now you can ask the customer about the value of this project. Is the project high value? What would make it high value? The value discussion is how you can identify potential return. It's still a guess, but a more educated guess.

> After due consideration of the risks of the calendar integration project, Dave and the rest of the IT directors decided to do just one two-week iteration on the project and see where they were after those two weeks.

Ranking with risk is not without problems. Sometimes you need more than one timebox to know about the relative risk of the project. Sometimes the customer insists the project is high value, without considering the other projects in the portfolio. In that case, you need to consult other people, such as all the project sponsors or all the customers, and explain that you can only do one of these projects. Under these circumstances, which project has the most value?

One aspect of assessing the project risk and return is to determine for how long a particular project is risky or has a potential return. A number of years ago, an organization wanted to put their client information in a secure area of their Web site. Security was a new field, and they weren't sure they knew everything they needed to do to keep the data confidential. Once a quarter, they tried to implement a feature in two weeks and test its security. As long as the other developers and testers could break the feature, the CIO decided the project was too risky. But about 18 months later, no one could break the features. Now the CIO moved the project up in the ranking because it was not too risky and had a much higher return.

Figure 1 shows how that organization reviewed the risks and the value.

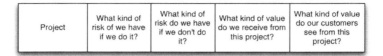

Project	What kind of risk of we have if we do it?	What kind of risk do we have if we don't do it?	What kind of value do we receive from this project?	What kind of value do our customers see from this project?

Figure 1:Rating a Project According to Risk and Value

When they reviewed the risks, they knew that if they didn't keep the information secure, they would be in trouble with their clients. They had few risks if they didn't do the project for a while. If the organization could implement the proper security, they would have a jump on their competition, but it would still be a selling job to their clients. Yet once the clients realized what they could do with their online information, the organization was sure they could change the way they worked with their clients.

Rank with Context

Sometimes, it's quite difficult to rank with points. It's especially difficult if you have different types of projects, which is quite common for IT departments. You might have "internal" projects to keep departments and systems up to date, as well as "external" projects that affect how you deliver products and services to your customers.

Table 4: Internal Projects, Ranked with Points

Internal Projects	Points
HR resume system	3000
Supply chain updates	2800
Year-end updated reports	2700
New reports for finance	200

One IT group first organized their projects and then ranked them as internal or external (see Table 4). In Table 4, you can see that the HR résumé system offers the highest value of the internal projects, but two of the other projects are not far behind. And in Table 5, all of the projects are ranked higher than the internal projects. This IT department had enough teams to fully staff two of the external projects and one of the internal projects.

Table 5: External Projects, Ranked with Points

External Projects	Points
Shopping cart additions	5000
Security for specific scenario	4500
Loyalty program, phase 1	3500

But separating the projects by type and ranking them helped the CIO explain to the different constituencies in the business why the IT group could not get to their project now. Once the senior management team saw the ranking, they could discuss the relative ranking and explain why different projects were ranked the way they were.

Pairwise Comparison and Double Elimination

There may be times when you need to look at every project in comparison to every other project; in other words, you need to do a pairwise comparison. Pairwise comparison is most useful when you have too many projects and not enough people to fully staff them. An easy way to do this is to write the name of every project on a stickie note, and place them all horizontally on a whiteboard or wall. Make sure you have all the necessary people in the room when you make the decisions. Once you've asked the "Should we do this project at all?" question, hold up two stickie notes and ask, "Which project is first, this one or that one?"

Double Elimination Tournament

Figure 2:Double Elimination is a type of Pairwise Comparison

As you decide which project is higher rank, put the stickies on the wall in vertical order, with the highest ranking sticky on the top. Now, take another sticky from your horizontal collection. Take the top sticky, and the new one, and ask, "Which one is first, this or that?" Put the top-most sticky on the wall, and pick up the next sticky, and ask the same question. Put the next sticky underneath the top-most sticky. Repeat until all the horizontal stickies are in vertical order. You now have the projects ranked in order.

Double elimination is a form of pairwise comparison. Many tennis tournaments are pairwise comparison, because the winners all play losers. Figure 2 is a picture of double elimination.

Because the winners of each round eventually are compared to the losers of each round, you have the opportunity to compare each project against each other project. Note that here the initial winner of the first round, Project 1 initially won against Project 2, but as the team discussed their reasons for each project's ranking, Project 2 did win against all the others and eventually prevailed.

Single elimination

Single elimination is a slightly easier approach to the project ranking, but does not compare each project against each other project.

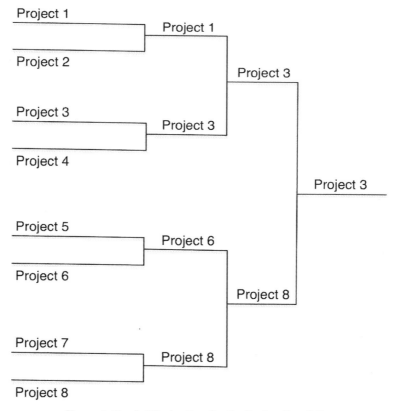

Figure 3: Single Elimination for the Project Portfolio

Use Your Mission and Values

You might find every ranking approach difficult to implement in your organization. Sometimes, that's because either you or senior management have not articulated your mission or have not defined the values of the organization. If either of those is true, the discussion about the ranking of each project might lead you in circles. In those circumstances, make sure you have defined you're your mission explicitly whether your mission is as a manager in your product development or IT organization, or as a C-level executive.

Once you know your mission, it's possible to use your mission to say yes this project is part of our mission. Or, your mission can tell you this project is not part of your mission. And, if you find that you have sacred cow projects, use your organization-defined values to describe why this project is a sacred cow and why you need to change that.

> As Dave was working through the projects, he discovered several people in Tanya's group were working on a data consolidation project. He asked Tanya what that project was. "It's a way to reduce the number of databases and disk drives in the organization," she replied.
>
> Dave thought for a minute, and asked, "When did this project start?"
>
> "As part of our green initiative," Tanya replied.
>
> Dave considered this and said, "Ok, we have a problem. One of our corporate values is to reduce waste. But this project is a lower priority and our green value is a lower priority than enabling the business to make money."

Tanya protested, "But when we save the company money, we make it easier for the money we make to go farther."

Dave explained, "Yes, you're right. And, *right now*, it's more important to make money than to save money. That's just for right now. I'm not saying we shouldn't do this project all. I am saying that for right now, we should not staff this project. That decision won't last forever, but for these next few iterations. Put the data consolidation project on the portfolio backlog and we'll reevaluate it the next time we review the whole portfolio."

If you do not have a mission for your organization or if you have not defined and articulated your values, your efforts to rank the portfolio will make the lack of mission or value articulation visible to you. If you have defined a mission and defined your corporate values, it will be easier to make the portfolio decisions. It still may not be easy, but the decisions will be clearer.

Ranking isn't Forever

Once you rank the portfolio, you only have to wait for one iteration to finish until you can re-rank the portfolio. Because you have that flexibility, it's easier to make the portfolio decisions, because you know the decision doesn't have to last any longer than an iteration's duration. Say your organization uses four-week iterations. If you need to make decisions faster, you can ask every project to move to two-week iterations. Now you have an opportunity every two weeks to re-evaluate the portfolio and know whether you want a team working on this project or not.

Remember to Kill Projects

Not every project deserves to stay on your backlog. Sometimes, products have had several releases (projects), and you've put another one on the backlog. Eventually you move it to the parking lot, because other projects are more valuable.

Even more important than moving projects out of the way are those projects that have completed some number of iterations, but are not providing value. When you rank them, they are lower than other projects you could be finishing. In that case, kill the project. Sure, you can take the leave-our-options route, and move the project to the backlog or the parking lot. But if you have a number of higher value projects and this one looks like it's never going to deliver that value, kill the project. You can always transform it in some other way if you want to start it up again.

Summary

Every leader and manager in the organization who has responsibility for staffing projects needs to rank the projects in his or her portfolio. You might be able to use a straightforward approach, and staff those projects.

More likely, you will need to make some decisions, and then re-evaluate the portfolio periodically. Use your corporate and department's mission and values to help guide your decisions. But the easiest way to make frequent-enough portfolio decisions is to work in relatively short timeboxes, implementing by feature and finishing work in that timebox. Now you have a product you can see and can reduce your portfolio decision risks.

References

1. Rothman, Johanna. *Manage Your Project Portfolio: Increase Your Capacity and Finish Your Projects,* Pragmatic Bookshelf, Raleigh NC and Dallas TX, 2009.

More from Jutta

I am working as an independent coach, consultant, and trainer. I have helped many teams and organizations all over the world to make the transition to an agile approach. I have a unique experience in applying agile processes within medium-sized to large distributed mission-critical projects. I focus also on techniques which help teach and learn and am a main lead in the pedagogical patterns project.

If you liked this book, you might like the other books I've written:

- Retrospectives for Organizational Change: An Agile Approach[27]
- Agile Software Development with Distributed Teams: Staying Agile in a Global World[28]
- Agile Software Development in the Large: Diving into the Deep[29]
- Pedagogical Patterns: Advice for Educators[30]

In addition, together with my partner Nicolai Josuttis, I have a (German) blog at Heise Developer:

- The World of IT[31]

---

[27]http://jeckstein.com/retrospectives
[28]http://jeckstein.com/index.php/distributed-teams
[29]http://jeckstein.com/agilebook
[30]http://jeckstein.com/index.php/ped-patts
[31]http://www.heise.de/developer/the-world-of-it-1296.html

I'd like to stay in touch either through my web site[32] or via social media. Please do invite me to connect with you on LinkedIn[33] or on Xing[34].

I would love to know what you think of this book. If you write a review of it somewhere, please let me know. Thanks!

---

[32]http://jeckstein.com

[33]https://de.linkedin.com/in/juttaeckstein

[34]http://www.xing.com/profile/Jutta_Eckstein

More from Johanna

I consult, speak, and train about all aspects of managing product development. I have a distinctly agile bent. I'm more interested in helping you become more effective than I am in sticking with some specific approach. There's a reason my newsletter is called the "Pragmatic Manager"—that's because I am!

If you liked this book, you might like the other books I've written:

- Agile and Lean Program Management: Scaling Collaboration Across the Organization[35]
- Predicting the Unpredictable: Pragmatic Approaches to Estimating Cost or Schedule[36]
- Manage Your Job Search[37]
- Hiring Geeks That Fit[38]
- Manage Your Project Portfolio: Increase Your Capacity and Finish More Projects[39]
- Manage It! Your Guide to Modern, Pragmatic Project Management[40]
- Behind Closed Doors: Secrets of Great Management[41]

In addition, I have essays in

---

[35]http://www.jrothman.com/books/agile-and-lean-program-management-scaling-collaboration-across-the-organization/

[36]http://www.jrothman.com/books/predicting-the-unpredictable-pragmatic-approaches-to-estimating-cost-or-schedule/

[37]http://www.jrothman.com/books/manage-your-job-search/

[38]http://www.jrothman.com/books/hiring-geeks-that-fit

[39]http://www.jrothman.com/books/manage-your-project-portfolio-increase-your-capacity-and-finish-more-projects/

[40]http://www.jrothman.com/books/manage-it-your-guide-to-modern-pragmatic-project-management/

[41]http://www.jrothman.com/books/behind-closed-doors-secrets-of-great-management/

- Readings for Problem-Solving Leadership[42]
- Center Enter Turn Sustain: Essays on Change Artistry[43]

I'd like to stay in touch with you. If you don't already subscribe, please sign up for my email newsletter, the Pragmatic Manager[44], on my web site. Please do invite me to connect with you on LinkedIn[45], and follow me on Twitter, @johannarothman.

I would love to know what you think of this book. If you write a review of it somewhere, please let me know. Thanks!

---

[42]https://leanpub.com/pslreader
[43]https://leanpub.com/changeartistry
[44]http://www.jrothman.com/pragmaticmanager/
[45]http://www.linkedin.com/in/johannarothman

Printed in Great Britain
by Amazon